SUPER CHARACTER DESIGN & POSES

Vol.2 HEROINE

by
YOU KUSANO

SUPER CHARACTER / DESIGN & POSES
Vol.2 HEROINE

by You Kusano ⓒ

Copyright ⓒ 2003 MPC Publishing Co., Ltd.

First original bilingual edition was published in 2001
by MPC Publishing Co., Ltd.
1-10-1, Uchi-kanda, Chiyoda-ku Tokyo 101-0047, Japan
URL : http://www.mpc-world.co.jp/

Author : You Kusano
Editing : Jun Itoh
DTP : Tsukuru Morita, Jun Itoh, Massan
Translasiton : Tsukuru Morita, Suzi Yamaguchi, Excite-kun

Distributor
Japan Publications Trading Co., Ltd.
1-2-1 Sarugaku-cho, Chiyoda-ku, Tokyo 101-0064, Japan
E-mail : jpt@jptco.co.jp
URL : http://www.jptco.co.jp/

First Printing : August 2003

ISBN4-88996-122-4
Printed in Japan

The main theme of this book is how to draw tough and hard-boiled characters and thier expressions, costumes, and arms. The collection of poses might be a reference guide for drawing your original work.

WORKS

This chapter shows the process for creating a new character. Based on a theme, this section focusses on the rough sketch until the finish. I have tried to summerize it so it is easily understood. I have included a variation of heroes from different genres and tried to recreate them as "hard" characters.

BODY

This chapter explains the basic stages of how to create a character. It includes how to draw the smart body indespensable to "super" characters. I have simply and effectively compared different variations of eyes and nose, and included paints regarding face and hair.

PEN&TECHNIQUE

Although this chapter seems small, we have edited it to include the necessary fundamental techniques which can be obtained easily with minimum effort.

POSES

This chapter as the name suggests, is a collection of poses. I think what makes this book attractive is the unification of technique and poses. This includes poses which are usually difficult to draw and about 200 commmonly drawn poses. As I am an illustrator, when I compiled this collection of poses I kept in mind "wouldn't it be great to have a collection of poses like this". Where possible, the characters that appear in this collection do not wear clothes. I have drawn them with a T-shirt or tank top so you can easily understand the body motion and form. You can add clothing and complete your own characters.

3

CONTENTS

ABOUT THIS BOOK · · · · · · · · · · · ·3

WORKS 5

KAREN · · · · · · · · · · · · · ·6

HARD COP · · · · · · · · · · · ·8

SF HARD · · · · · · · · · · · ·10

PAPILLON · · · · · · · · · · · ·12

WILD GIRL · · · · · · · · · ·14

STREET GANG · · · · · · · · · ·16

LOVELY GIRL · · · · · · · · ·18

FANTASY · · · · · · · · · · · ·20

SEALA THE WITCH · · · · · · ·22

ALIEN WOMAN · · · · · · · · ·24

MARIA THE SUPER HEROINE · · ·26

BODY 29

SUPER BODY · · · · · · · · · ·30

SIDE & BACK · · · · · · · · · ·31

BODIES · · · · · · · · · · · ·32

UNDERSTANDING BODY · · · · ·34

BREAST · · · · · · · · · · · ·36

HIP · · · · · · · · · · · · · ·38

ARM · · · · · · · · · · · · · ·39

LEG · · · · · · · · · · · · · ·40

FACE 41

ANGLE · · · · · · · · · · · ·42

EYE · · · · · · · · · · · · · ·43

NOSE · · · · · · · · · · · · ·45

MOUTH · · · · · · · · · · · ·47

THE SHAPE OF FACE · · · · · · ·49

UNDERSTANDING FACE · · · · · ·50

HAIR STYLE · · · · · · · · · ·51

CHARACTERIZATION 53

SMALL BUT STRONG · · · · · · · ·54

POWER INSIDE · · · · · · · · ·55

COSTUME · · · · · · · · · · · ·56

SPECIAL EFFECT · · · · · · · ·57

FEATURE · · · · · · · · · · · ·58

THE WORK · · · · · · · · · · ·59

PEN&TECHNIQUE 61

PEN · · · · · · · · · · · · · ·62

OBLIQUE STROKES · · · · · · · ·64

SOLID · · · · · · · · · · · · ·65

ONE POINT ADVICE · · · · · · ·66

ZOOM · · · · · · · · · · · · ·68

POSES 69

Super Character's
WORKS

KAREN

This cool girl is a professional killer.
She is a killing machine who
belongs to a certain secret
organization.
She is about 20 years old and has a
cool expression.
She is a modern day lady.

1 one A cool beautiful girl. This is the main theme.

I wanted to give her
a sharp look
so I narrowed the
width of her head
and gave her a
straight hairstyle.

She has long straight blond
hair with a cool expression.
It's decided!

2 two If we dress her in fashionable clothes
this character is complete.

Stylish props
and senses
suit her.

It is fun to dress her in
various fashionable outfits
for different scenes.

3 three Completion

This time a
black mini
dress
completes her
look.

KAREN

■WORKS■

HARD COP

She is one of the stereotype "tough" heroines.
She is a hard action female detective.
Let's create a heroine who is a lone wolf.
She loves justice and hates authority.

1 one She has beautiful blond hair. That is it!

Sunglasses are absolutely required.

2 two Her clothes were already decided in my mind.
Leather trousers and a black coat.
I worried about what to put underneath,
a high neck, tank top. There is lots to choose
I decided on a crew neck.

A tank top with an open front. It is the sexiest.

A high neck is smart but not sexy.

Although everyone has their own preference I decided on the T-shirt on the right.

■WORKS■

SF HARD

I made a heroine for a science fiction like Star Wars.
She is about 18 years old.
She is a hidden ability which enables her to save mankind.
She wears a combat uniform.

1 one Pay attention to her age. She is 18 years old. She has a charming but fearless image.

It is somewhat common and there is no brightness.

Sexiness is emphasized by her eyes lifted up a little. I chose this one.

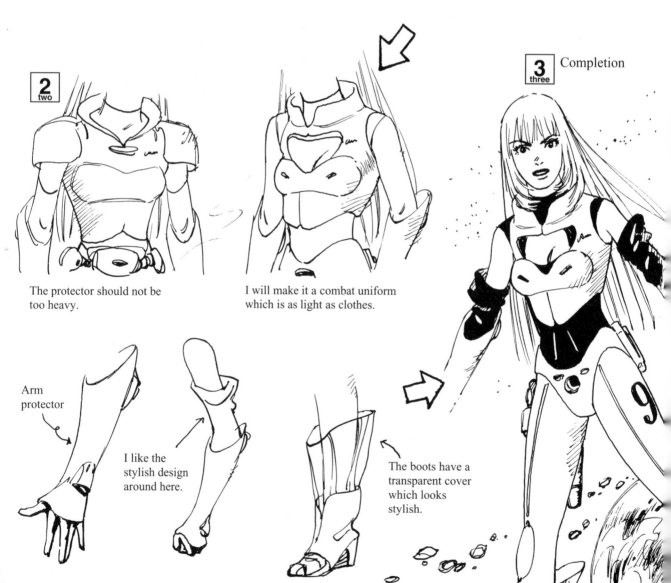

2 two

The protector should not be too heavy.

I will make it a combat uniform which is as light as clothes.

3 three Completion

Arm protector

I like the stylish design around here.

The boots have a transparent cover which looks stylish.

PAPILLON

A female version Lupin.
Let's call her "Thief
Papillon".
A sexy and smart
character is made.

1 one   I want her to be gorgeous. I am thinking about giving her a mask. It will most likely become her distinctive feature.

Papillon means butterfly. Her mask will be like a butterfly.

I want to also make her hair style as gorgeous as this.

2 two   The problem is her costume. I want her costume to be sexy but to have punch.

Add metal ornaments in some parts.

I am considering a tight fitting body suits. I want her bodyline to be slender and beautiful.

3 three   Completion

Metal ornaments designed by Papillon are attached to the buckle of her belt and tips of her boots. Cool!

PAPILLON

WILD GIRL

This is a tale set in the near future of a war between aliens and the remaining survivors after the earth was destroyed. The heroine is a lone wolf who fights the aliens.

Although this is set in the wilderness there is also an underground city.

1 one   When you think of a wild person, you tend to imagine a manlike character, so I made her sexy.

This type is also good.

I used Marilyn Monroe's image as my concept.

2 two   I considered a jacket but based on a tank top to emphasize the woman.

Tatoo

The shirt is cut short.

Trousers are baggy work trousers.

She finds some men's army pants and wears them. It shows a world where material things are insufficient.

Many accessories are attached to the body to show how desperate the situation is.

3 three

WILD GIRL

STREET GANG

She detests big organizations such as the mafia.
She is a lone wolf who fundamentally doesn't belong to any particular gang but she does team up with small gangs sometimes.

1 one I want to create a face which shows her strong willed personality.

This ia too legitimate.

I decided to go with this face and this gorgeous hair. Her accessories are flashy.

2 two

Sunglasses are too common.

While drawing many sketches I decided on the conbination of a cap and goggles. A pierced earing in her nose would also be good.

3 three Completion

Tatoo

Stylish accessories

Protecter

I combined a T-shirt, tank top and track pants.

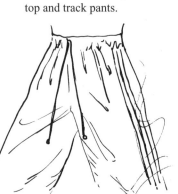

I combined a tight fitted workout tank top with a loose tank top on top.

STREET GANG

LOVELY GIRL

This SF story is set in a time when time travel is done freely.

This is a heroine story set in space on relay station which is also a bar.

She is the station master as well as the bar manager.

She has a tail which has hidden power.

This is a hard story which is sexy and stylish.

1 one Sexy and stylish. Be sure to incorporate a stationmaster's image.

A regulation cap will probably be an element of her image.

I tried an American police cap. Very cool!

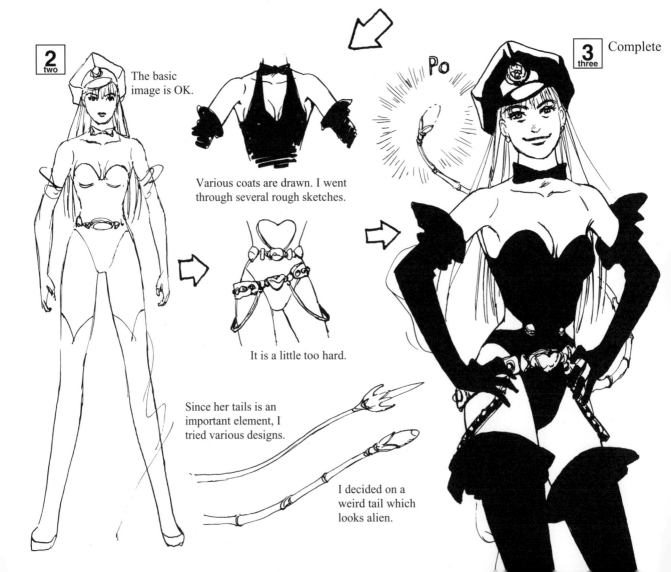

2 two The basic image is OK.

Various coats are drawn. I went through several rough sketches.

It is a little too hard.

Since her tails is an important element, I tried various designs.

I decided on a weird tail which looks alien.

3 three Complete

Po

LOVELY GIRL

FANTASY

This is a fateful story about an angel-like girl who gets into trouble with the mafia.
It is set in the present day.
The heroine is a gentle innocent girl about 18 years old.
It's OK to create on ordinary, bright and healthy girl.

1 one I imagined an ordinary, bright and healthy high school girl.

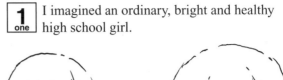

This image is too young.

Her eyes are gentle and she doesn't wear much make-up. I chose this one.

2 two She wears everyday 18 year old clothes.

Her costume will be changed occationally for some scenes.

SEALA THE WITCH

As the title suggests, she is a witch.
She is not an old witch with a bent nose. She is a young and beautiful witch. She is wild but sexy.

1 one The main theme is a wild but sexy witch. I think her hairstyle is an important element.

2 two Let's think about her costume. A mantle is needed.

It is a cool mantle.

What should we do around her neck.

3 three Complete

I tried a hood. Great! Just how I imagined her.

The trench coat came into my mind immediately, and I decided on the design for the portion around the neck.

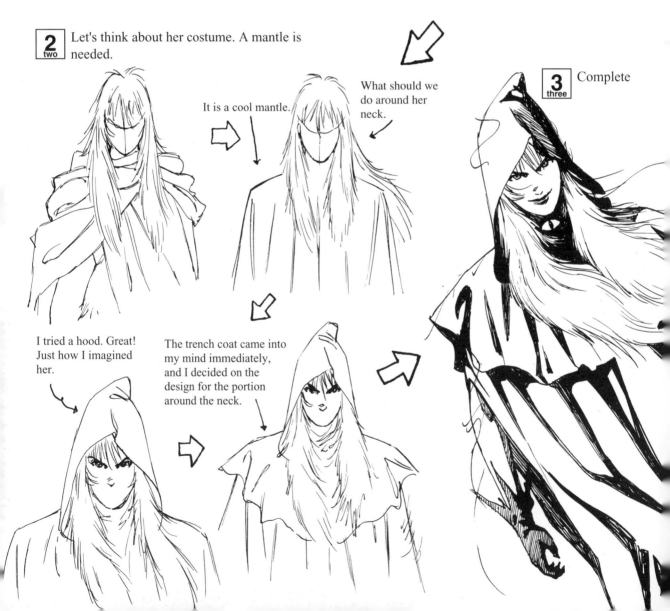

ALIEN WOMAN

She is the only monstar in this book.

I made a wild alien female fighter. Although she is a monster, she still needs a feminine image so I have created a beautiful but cool monster.

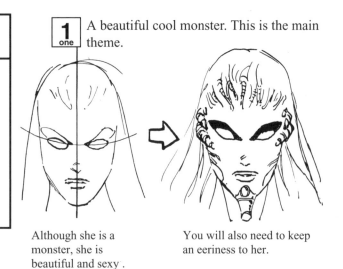

1 one A beautiful cool monster. This is the main theme.

Although she is a monster, she is beautiful and sexy .

You will also need to keep an eeriness to her.

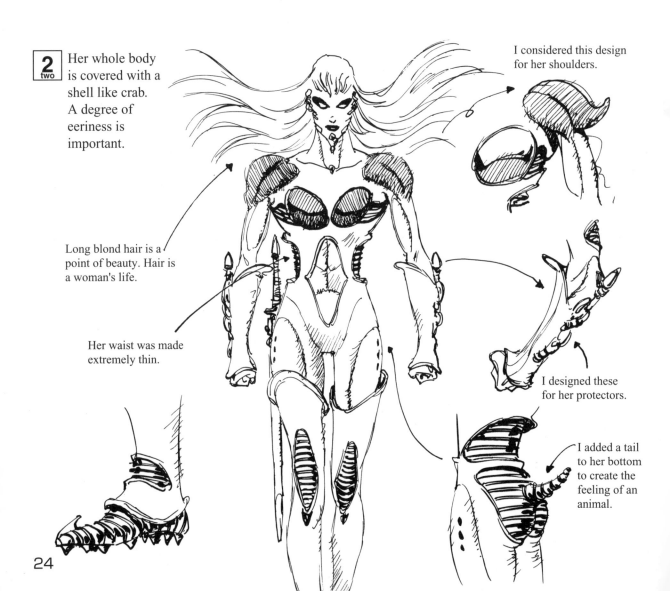

2 two Her whole body is covered with a shell like crab. A degree of eeriness is important.

I considered this design for her shoulders.

Long blond hair is a point of beauty. Hair is a woman's life.

Her waist was made extremely thin.

I designed these for her protectors.

I added a tail to her bottom to create the feeling of an animal.

ALIEN WOMAN

MARIA THE SUPER HEROINE

This character is one of the stereotype heroines. She is the female version of Superman. she is a SF heroine who flies through the air with supernatural powers. You can have fun designing her costume because there are so many different options. Let's give her a mantle.

1 one   She has a cute character and beautiful face.

This was already decided. I wanted a healthy and intellectual feeling to her.

2 two   Next it is costume design.

Various lengths of her gloves were considered.

3 three   Completion

It seems that a protector is better than a body suit.

The protector was attached on her shoulders.

Her weapon A round boomerang

I tried a miniskirt but it made her look too much like Superwoman.

Long boots.

MARIA
THE SUPER HEROINE

Super Character's
BODY

■BODY■

SUPER BODY

It is rather difficult to draw a smart female body. However, if you memorize the illustration on the right, you will be able to draw it easily.

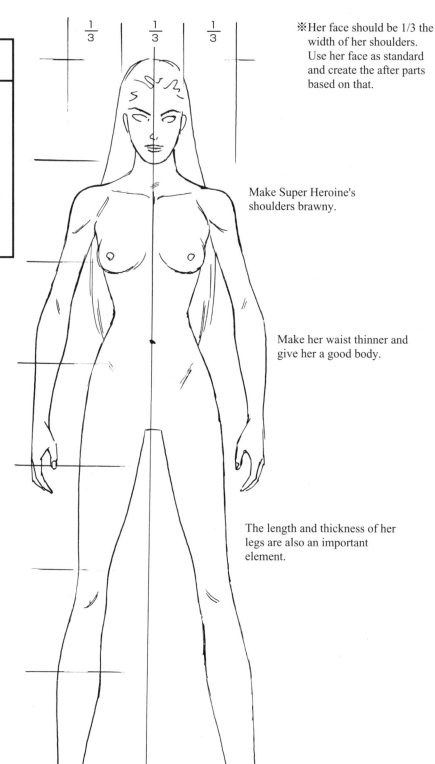

$\frac{1}{3}$ $\frac{1}{3}$ $\frac{1}{3}$

※Her face should be 1/3 the width of her shoulders. Use her face as standard and create the after parts based on that.

Make Super Heroine's shoulders brawny.

Make her waist thinner and give her a good body.

※It is sexier not to draw too much muscle. Look at and study women's magazines etc.

The length and thickness of her legs are also an important element.

Standard nude

SIDE&BACK

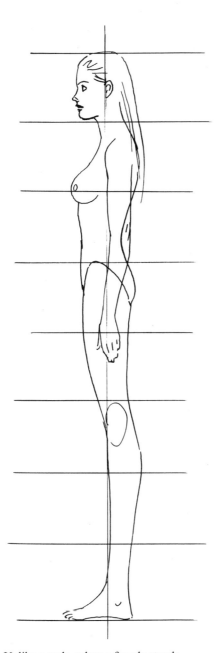

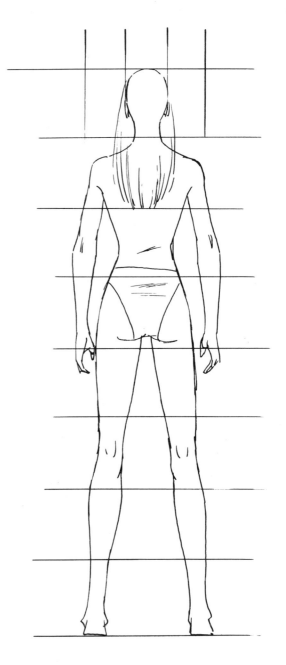

Unlike a male, when a female stands
stretching her breast out, she is
beautiful.

※Let's make a beautiful body by making sure the width of
her shoulders and thickness of legs are the same seen
from the front, back and side.

BODIES

Compared with P36, it is a more macho body.

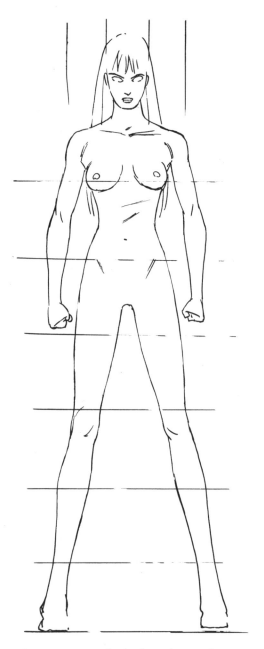

Compared with P36, it is a more feminine body.

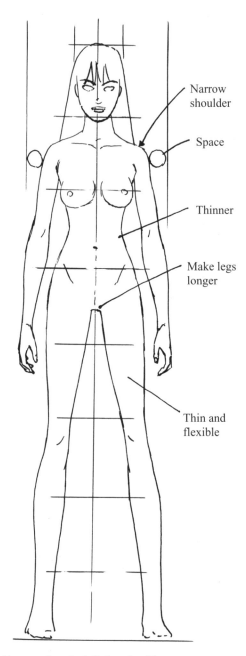

Narrow
shoulder

Space

Thinner

Make legs
longer

Thin and
flexible

I want you to emphasize brawniness and increase the breadth of her shoulders more than on the standard body on P36.

Compared to the left, her shoulders are round and gentle. Other portions of her body are much finer.

More macho   More feminine

Let's compare the two upper figures.
The difference between a wild image and a feminine
image should be noticed.

■BODY■

UNDERSTANDING BODY

Use fashion and nude magazines as a reference, and you will understand the sexy motion.

A A lady-like motion

The breast is thin.

Figure A has a crooked breast.

The male in figure B has a thick breast so it does not bend.

B Manly motion

Thick breast

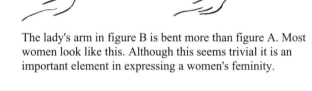

The lady's arm in figure B is bent more than figure A. Most women look like this. Although this seems trivial it is an important element in expressing a women's feminity.

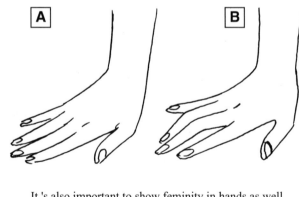

It 's also important to show feminity in hands as well. You can capture a lady's beauty by bending the fingers a little as in figure B. However, be careful not to overdo it as it then becomes unnatural.

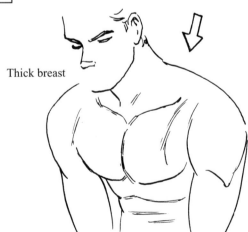

●The movement of a women's body●

■BODY■
BREAST

To draw a female body realistically, it is important to include her breasts.

A Correct

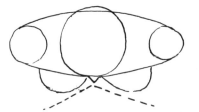

When seen from above, it spreads horizontally.

B Incorrect

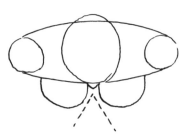

Do not use this except when you want to exaggerate her breasts.

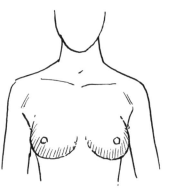

A is a natural bust.

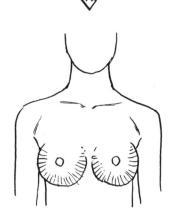

If seen from the front her breasts look unnatural.

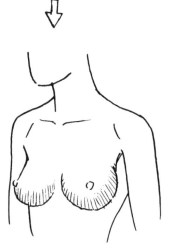

A is a natural bust even when seen diagonally.

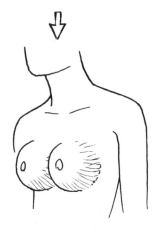

It is unnatural and looks swollen.

■BODY■
BREAST

Let's see how to show her bust in tight fitting clothes and loose shirts.

1 one — When she wears a fight fitting shirt it is pulled by the bulging on both sides of the bust. Therefore wrincles appear sideways.

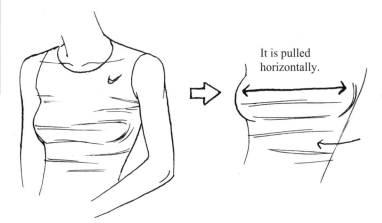

It is pulled horizontally.

2 two — She has a somewhat looser shirt on. It starts from the tip of a bust and creates slack wrinkles.

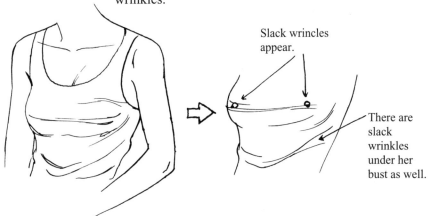

Slack wrincles appear.

There are slack wrinkles under her bust as well.

3 three — She has a blouse on. Vertical wrinkles appear around the tip of a bust.

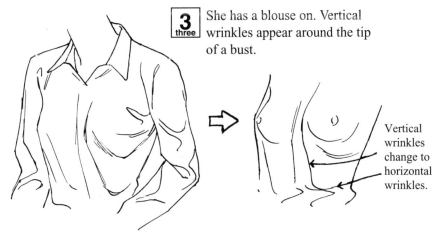

Vertical wrinkles change to horizontal wrinkles.

■BODY■

HIP

Charming hips are an important element. Whether she's wearing jeans or a skirt if you understand the basic shape of the hip, it will make it easier to draw difficult hiplines.

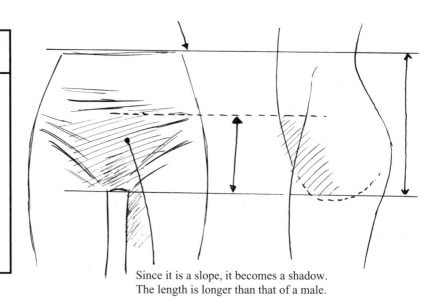

Since it is a slope, it becomes a shadow. The length is longer than that of a male.

If the figure on the right is shown diagrammatically, it will look like the figure on the left.

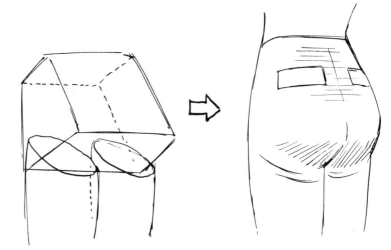

Man

Woman

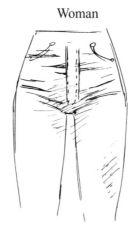

When wearing a skirt

ARM

Let's understand the structure of the arm.

Seen from the side, it is wide.

Seen from the front, it is narrow.

Seen from the front, it is horizontally broad.

※Let's be cautious of the difference between the upper structure and lower structure from the elbow.

LEG

Let's understand the
structure of legs.

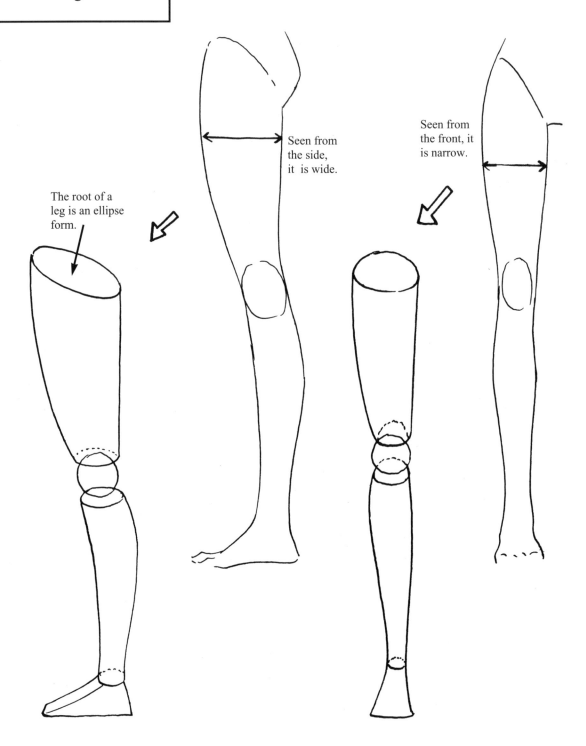

The root of a
leg is an ellipse
form.

Seen from
the side,
it is wide.

Seen from
the front, it
is narrow.

Super Character's
FACE

■FACE■

ANGLE

Let's study the face seen from various angles using an egg. As shown in a right figure, a line is drawn on the surface of an egg, and an eye, a nose, and a mouth are drawn. Let's study how the face changes when seen from above, the side and diagonally.

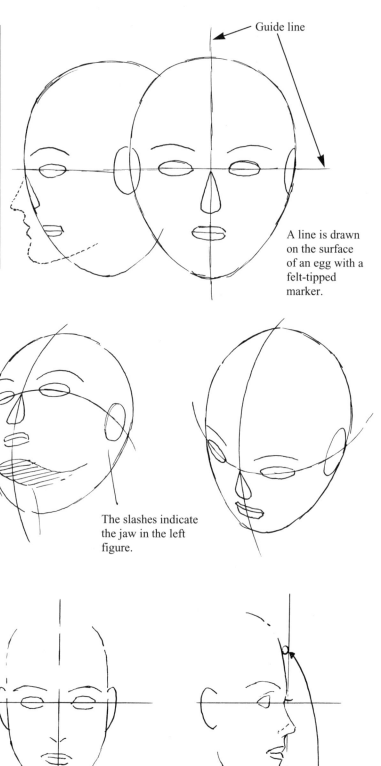

Guide line

A line is drawn on the surface of an egg with a felt-tipped marker.

The slashes indicate the jaw in the left figure.

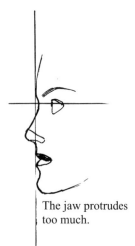

The jaw protrudes too much.

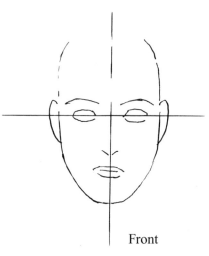

Front

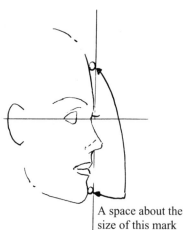

Side

A space about the size of this mark makes a beautiful profile.

42

■FACE■
EYE

The eyes are the most important features when drawing a woman. It can be said that all the features of a face are decided by the eyes. I will show you some tips for creating beautiful eyes.

The space between the eyes should be the width of one eye. Of course, fine tuning is required.

The position of the eye for a profile should be similar to the figure below.

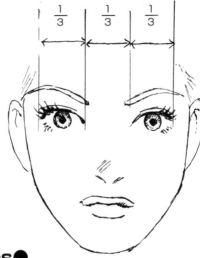

●The position of eyes●

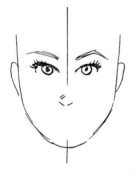

The eyes are too close.

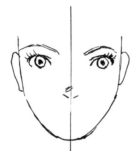

The eyes are too far apart.

Too sunken

Too far forward

Well defined eyes are typical of Caucasians.

Eyes typical of Asian people

43

●The size of eyes●

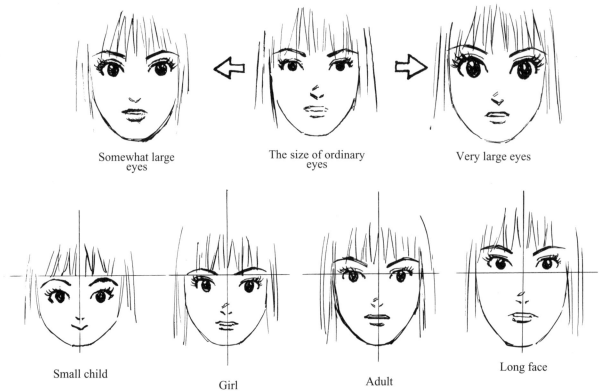

Somewhat large eyes

The size of ordinary eyes

Very large eyes

Small child

Girl

Adult

Long face

●Various eyes●

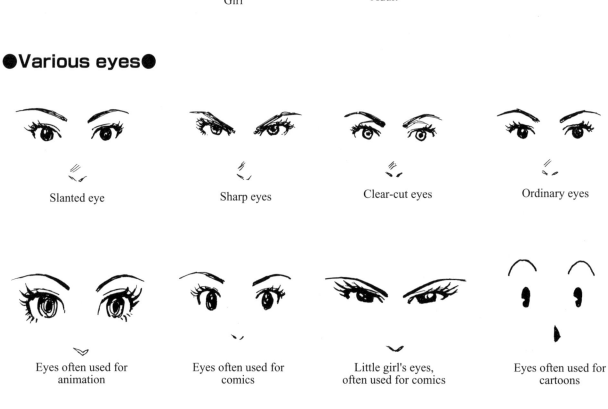

Slanted eye

Sharp eyes

Clear-cut eyes

Ordinary eyes

Eyes often used for animation

Eyes often used for comics

Little girl's eyes, often used for comics

Eyes often used for cartoons

■FACE■

NOSE

I'm sure there are lots of people who are not good at drawing noses. It is difficult to draw a nose especially from the front. If it's not cute and if you draw it too simple its hard to balance the other parts.

●The position of noses●

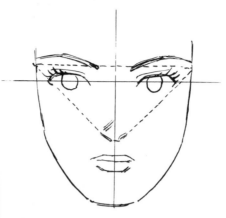

Maintain balance with an equilateral triangle.

Use the eyes as a guideline, the size and positioning is just right in the picture above.

●The length of noses●

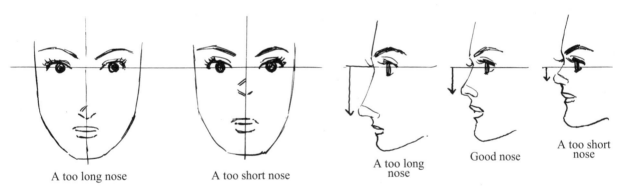

A too long nose

A too short nose

A too long nose

Good nose

A too short nose

You can create an distinctive character by intentionally shortening or lengthening the nose. I want to introduce some examples in the right figures.

A short large nose

A long nose

A short nose

NOSE

●The variation of noses●

Let's try drawing noses using various methods.

Only draw the
head of the
nose.

The nose is shown
by shadowing the
bridge and under
the nose.

Shown by shading

Shown by simplified
shading

●Various noses●

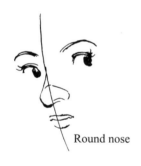

Round nose

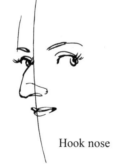

Hook nose

Square nose

Thin nose

Standard nose

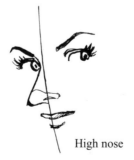

High nose

Low nose

A upward nose

MOUTH

The mouth is the 2nd most important part after the eyes. The role of the mouth is important in expressing sensuality, cuteness etc.

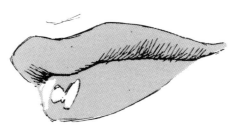

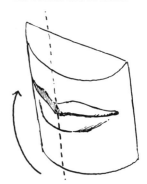

The central line of a face

The right edge of the mouth is hidden.

※It is easy to understand if you imagine the mouth is attached to a stand as shown in the right figure. Draw it on a round cylinder and be careful it doedn't turn out flat.

A smiling mouth seen from the front. The right figure shows the same smiling mouth from the side.

●Various mouths seen from front●

MOUTH

●The variation of mouths●

THE SHAPE OF FACE

●The shape of face●

Even with the exact same eyes, her look totally changes with different shape of the face.

●Various faces●

UNDERSTANDING FACE

●Faces from above●

●Faces from below●

 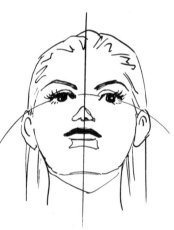 

●Faces from back●

HAIR STYLE

Hairstyle is more imoprtant on females than males.
You probably think that drawing hair is just drawing lines.
But actually it is quite difficult because you need to capture the flow of the hair.
Let's study different ways of expressing hair.

It is important not to draw too many lines. Let's keep it to the necessary minimum.

●Arrange Hair lines●

There are too many lines.

OK

There are too many lines.

OK

Super Character's

Super Character's
CHARACTERIZATION

SMALL BUT STRONG

Although toughness is mostly shown through appearance, you can also enhance this toughness by how you position the character.

A A ordinary big character. The body is big and power is expressed throughout the whole body.

B Although she is a girl she has a mysterious hidden ability which produces fierceness.

POWER INSIDE

A character may seem gentle but becomes violent when inner emotions are revealed.

■Original■ ■Hard■

■Original■

■Hard■

■CHARACTERIZATION■
COSTUME

Depending on the design of costume, it becomes a novelty and it can make the character very attractive. It is a very important technique.

■Original■

■CHARACTERIZATION■
SPECIAL EFFECT

●The variation of expression●

In order to draw a character, you have to be able to use various characters and expressions properly. If sexiness and loveliness can be expressed, that is fine.

COOL WOMAN

PRETTY GIRL

SEXY WOMAN

CRAZY WOMAN

THE WORK

I made examples of physique, character, costume, effects and expressions. I hope you are able to use this as a reference.

Super Character's
PEN&TECHNIQUE

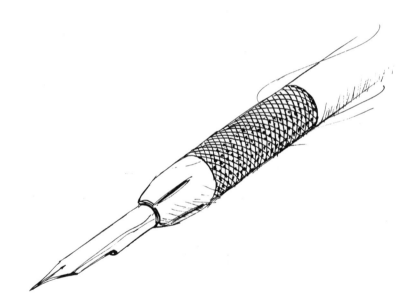

■PEN&TECHNIQUE■

PEN

I mainly use a circle pen for drafting. The circle pen is hard and can draw very thin lines and very thick lines. If you sharpen it on a whetstone, it draws line new again. It is practical and economical pen.

●The variation of pens●

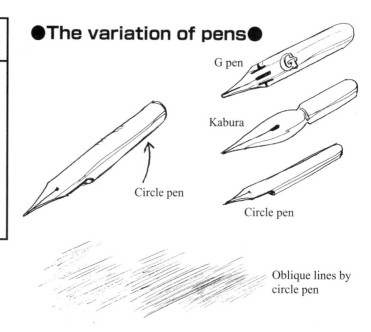

G pen

Kabura

Circle pen

Circle pen

Oblique lines by circle pen

●The line drawn with the circle pen

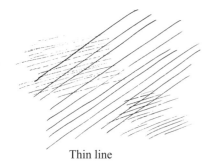

Thin line

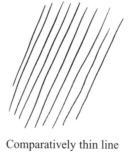

Comparatively thin line

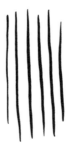

Thick line

Very thick line

KMT kent 150kg

Kent for comics

BLACK

●Paper
It is important to choose the right paper so that the pen doesn't catch on the paper. Test various types and choose the one that suits you. I use 150kg KMK Kent.

●Ink
Water resistant ink is better because it does melt and run when using white correction fluid. I use black from Holbein waterproof color inks.

62

■PEN&TECHNIQUE■

PEN

In order to master the circle pen you will need to practice. Compared to other pens it is quite strong.
However, once you get used to it, it is an exellent pen and you won't be able to part with it.

●The variation of expression by circle pen●

A An illustration drawn with a thin line

B An illustration combining thin and thick lines

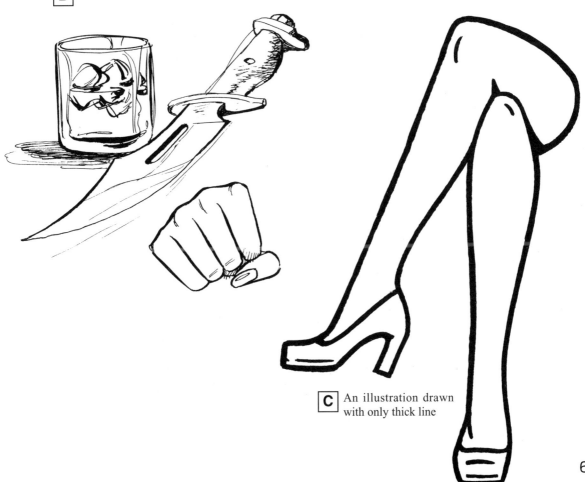

C An illustration drawn with only thick line

■PEN&TECHNIQUE■

OBLIQUE STROKES

Use the oblique strokes mainly to achieve a cubic effect and the feeling of quality.

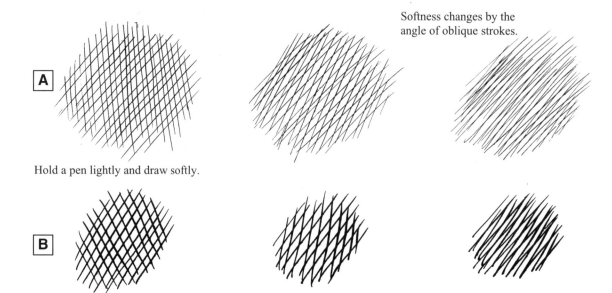

Softness changes by the angle of oblique strokes.

A

Hold a pen lightly and draw softly.

B

B is almost ineffective except for special usage.

■Texture example■

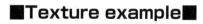

Dustcloth

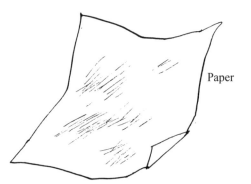

Paper

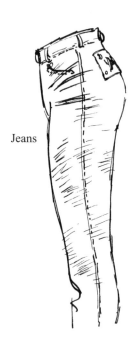

Jeans

The flow of a slash is arranged when drawing a griddle.

Many things were expressed by using touches in practice A. Establish your own expression.

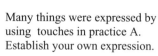

Let's draw oblique lines well without crossing them.

■PEN&TECHNIQUE■

SOLIDITY

A This is often used in American comics.

B By one thin line

C It is drawn by crossing lines. You can see that the thinner the lines the more realistic it becomes.

■Texture example■

Arm

Wrinkles of cloth.

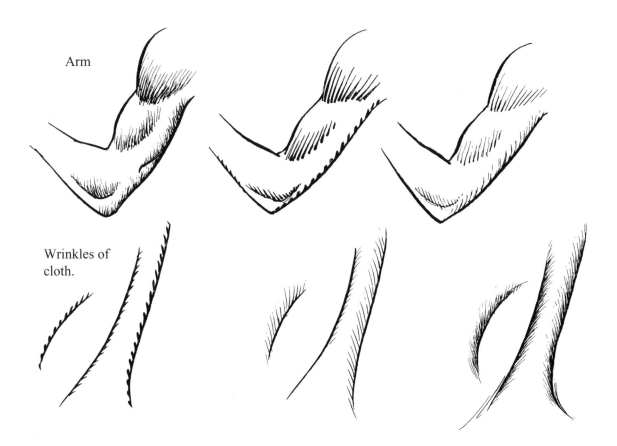

ONE POINT ADVICE

1 one Buy one Figure super heroine!

If you have Superwoman or Catwoman, practice drawing a body by referring to this figure.

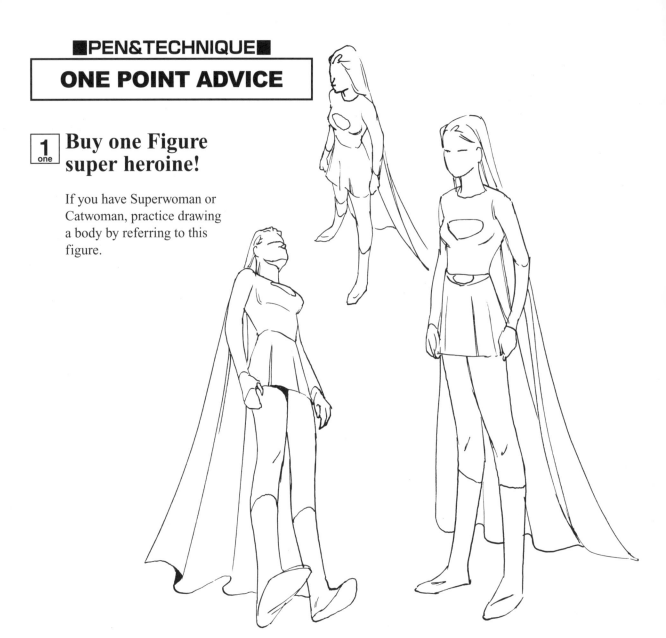

2 two Refer to reference material!

When drawing bodies refer to fashion or nude magazines. When drawing mechanics refer to motercycle or car magazines.

3 three | Use a mirror!

It is very convenient if you always prepare a mirror on your desk. It is useful especially when drawing a hand. You can draw a hand holding a glass etc, while looking at it in the mirror.

4 four | You can make a character more powerful !

by exaggerating one portion of the same pose.

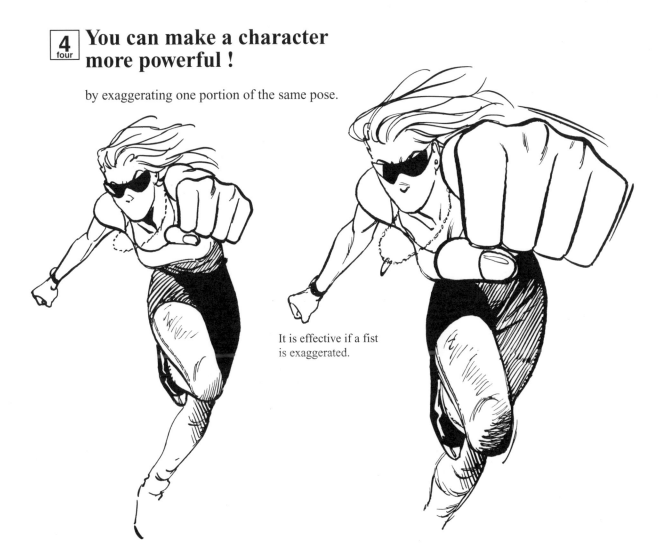

It is effective if a fist is exaggerated.

ZOOM

The more exaggerated, the more effective.
I compared the lower figures.

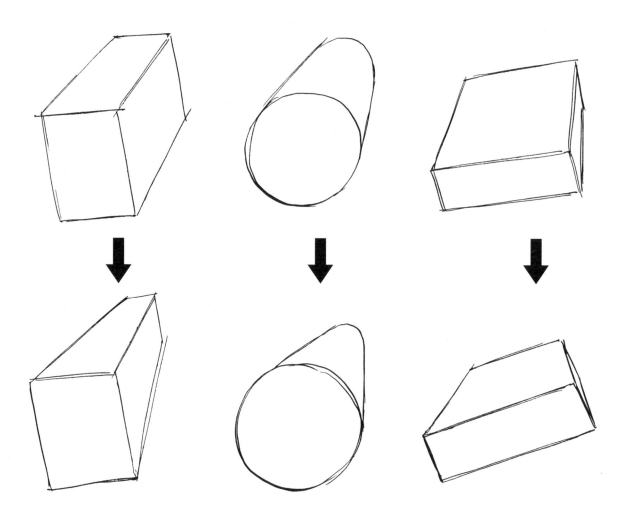

As shown in the left example, force changes by how it is exaggerated. If it is actually used in an illustration or comic it will turn out like the left example.

Super Character's
POSES

WALK

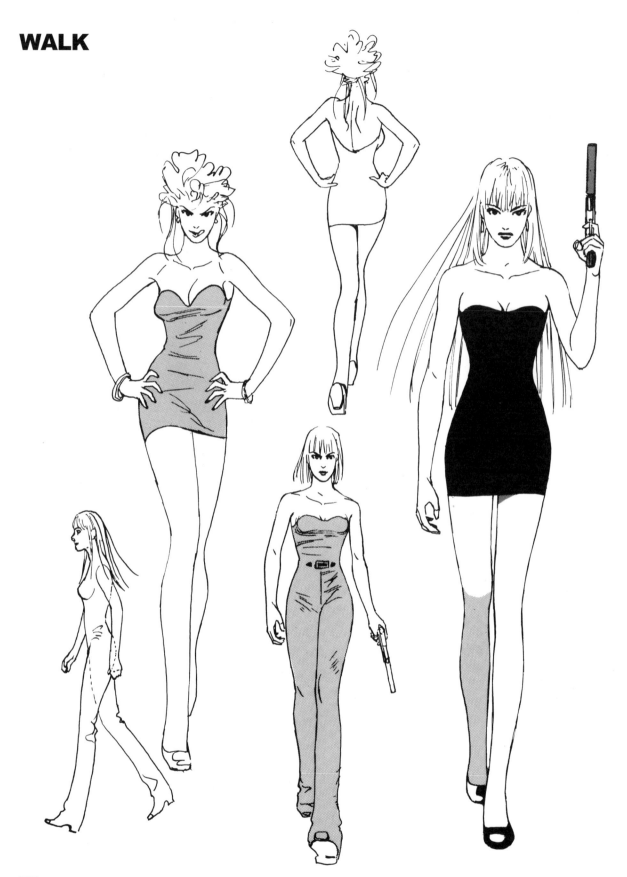

RUN

PUNCH

KICK

KICK

BLADE

FLY

SHOT

SEXY

SEXY

SEXY

RIFLE

95

SHOWER

SHOWER

DIVING

KISS

COOL

DRIVE

DRIVE

※This is a format for cars. I think this is easy to use if you trace this format then add the body of the car you like.

PHONE

BICYCLE

DRINK

Coats are often used on action heroes.

Long black coats are very cool.

There are a lot of coats appearing in this POSE section so please refer to them.

Loosely worn over the shoulders. It is draped to look like a mantle unbuttoned so it flutters in the wind cool.

■POSE■

JACKET

Suits are an important fashion for grown-up women and they often accompany tough women.
Understand the structure of suits and you will want to learn to draw them. Look at fashion magazines etc and study.

Since it contains pads, the shoulder is wide.

It looks smarter if the waist is tight.

The collar is pulled by right and left.

If an arm is moved, the shoulder will rise.

The collar has also been pulled.

If a hand is raised, the bottom side will be pulled up.

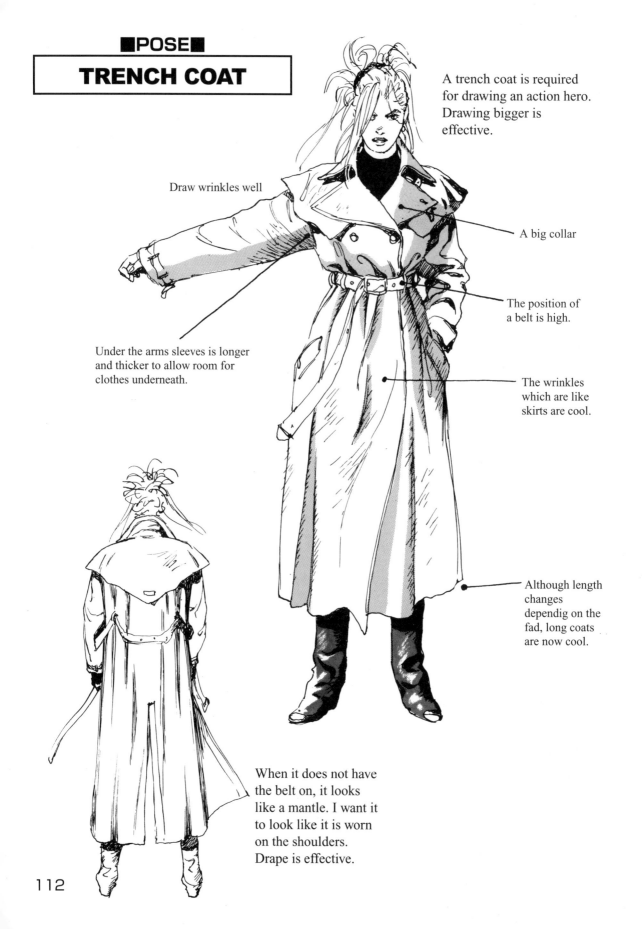

■POSE■
TRENCH COAT

A trench coat is required for drawing an action hero. Drawing bigger is effective.

Draw wrinkles well

A big collar

The position of a belt is high.

Under the arms sleeves is longer and thicker to allow room for clothes underneath.

The wrinkles which are like skirts are cool.

Although length changes dependig on the fad, long coats are now cool.

When it does not have the belt on, it looks like a mantle. I want it to look like it is worn on the shoulders. Drape is effective.

TRENCH COAT

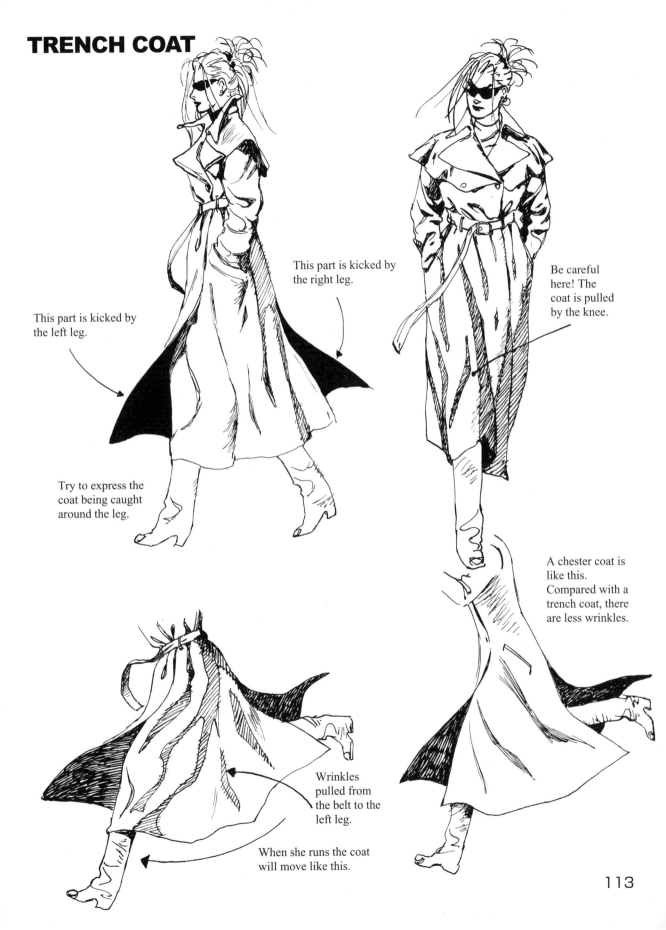

This part is kicked by the right leg.

This part is kicked by the left leg.

Try to express the coat being caught around the leg.

Be careful here! The coat is pulled by the knee.

A chester coat is like this. Compared with a trench coat, there are less wrinkles.

Wrinkles pulled from the belt to the left leg.

When she runs the coat will move like this.

HAND

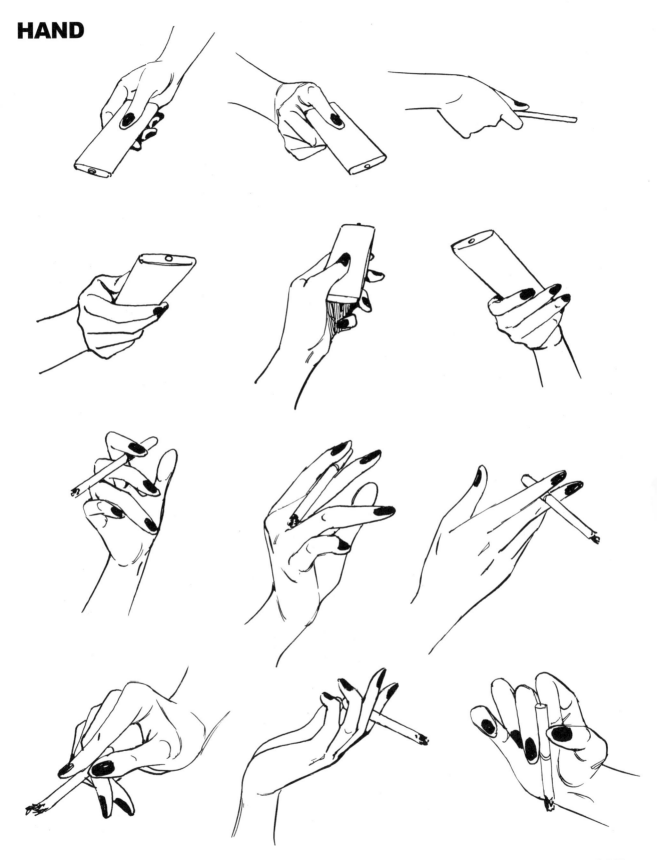

HAND

HAND

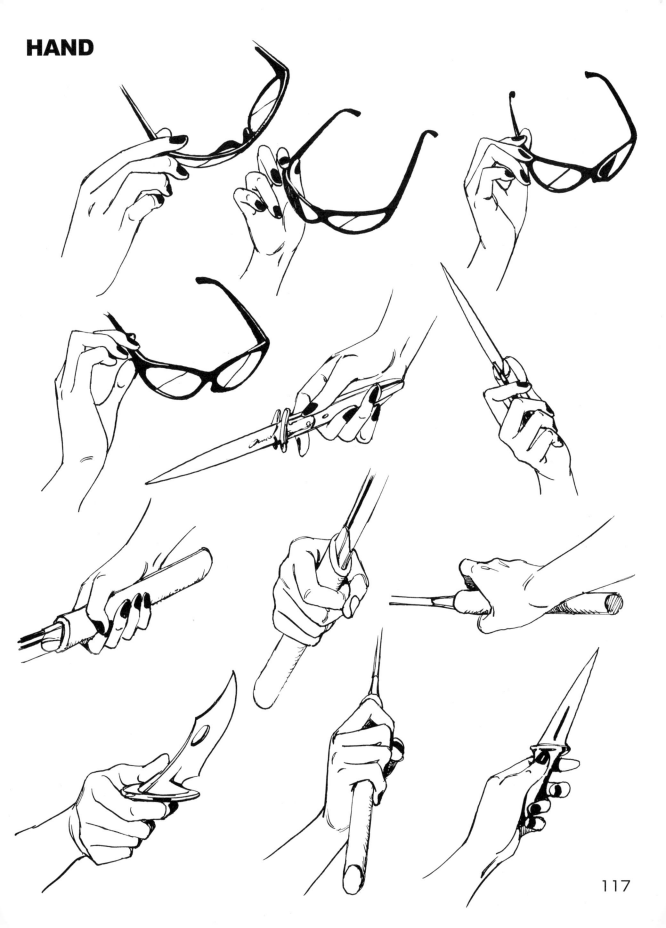

HAND

HAND

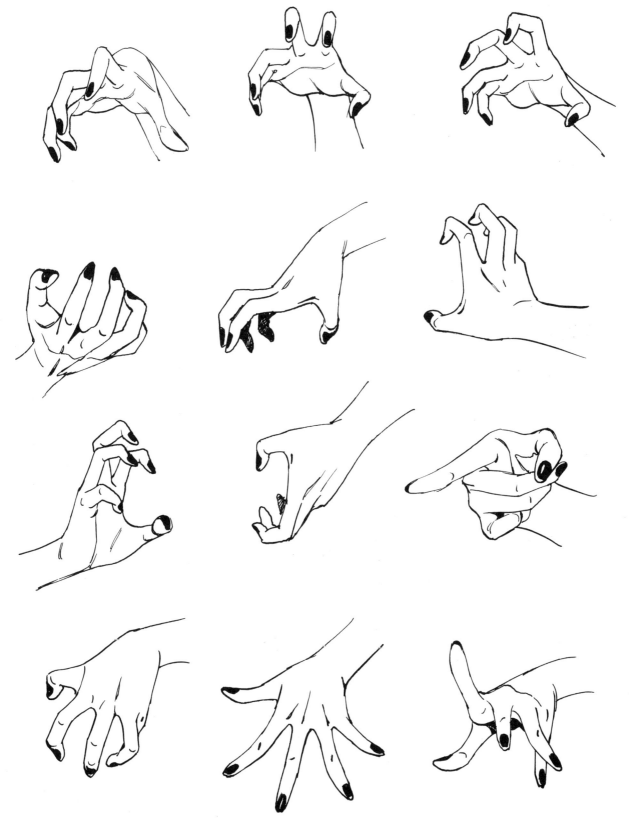